BLESSING YOUR CHILDREN

in Prayer and Faith

COPYRIGHT

ISBN: 979-8-218-33320-1
Printed in the United States of America
© 2023 by Victory Life Publishing
PO Box 427
Durant, OK 74702
dsm@pastorduane.com
580.634.5665

CONTENTS

INTRODUCTION

"... And the Lord spake unto Moses, saying, Speak unto Aaron and unto his sons, saying, On this wise ye shall bless the children of Israel, saying unto them, The Lord bless thee, and keep thee: The Lord make his face shine upon thee, and be gracious unto thee: The Lord lift up his countenance upon thee, and give thee peace.

NUMBERS 6:22-26 (KJV)

We see here in Numbers how the high priest (Aaron) and his sons (spiritual authorities) were instructed to bless God's people by speaking over them. They spoke the blessing and favor of the Lord. This is how we bless our children as parental authority over them. We are to speak God's promises and loving kindness over their lives. Why?

The blessing of the Lord, it maketh rich, and he addeth no sorrow with it.

PROVERBS 10:22 (KJV)

Things are not blessings; however, they can become blessings. The "blessing of the Lord" is an intangible thing that when mixed with faith affects tangible things. Blessing children is a biblical principle that is throughout both the Old and New Testaments and one we need to practice in our lives.

1

God blesses us as His children and desires that we pass that on to our children and grandchildren for generations.

Throughout scripture we see **two primary ways** that God blesses us:

1. **The spoken word of God over us bestowing favor and affirmations. God's promises are blessings that He performs in our lives when acted upon in faith. Speak God's word and promises over your children.**

2. **The laying on of hands. Physical touch is important especially when praying God's promises over your children. Include hugs, holding hands, putting them on your lap, etc. This communicates love, warmth, and commitment.**

Both our words and touch are important in communicating love, acceptance, and value to our children. The following scriptures are examples of both these methods in transferring blessings:

- Issac blessed his son Jacob in *Genesis 27:28-29* - How? By speaking divine favor and prosperity over him.

- Israel (Jacob) blessed his grandsons Ephraim and Manasseh in *Genesis 48:9, 13-20* – How? By speaking a blessing of favor and God's divine prosperity.

- Moses blessed Joshua (a spiritual son) in *Numbers 27:18-23* – How? By transferring honor and some of his

2

authority to him by laying hands on him and speaking over him.

- Jesus blessed children in *Mark 10:16* – How? He hugged them, laid hands on them, and spoke blessings over them.

- Paul blessed Timothy (a spiritual son) in *2 Timothy 1:6* – How? He laid hands on him and prophesied over him.

This booklet is designed to be used as a devotional guide. Each topic will assist you in sharing biblical promises made by God for you and your children. Apply these scriptures to bless your children and share God's love for them.

How to use this booklet as a devotional outline **(5 helpful suggestions):**

1. **Keep it simple** – Read one scripture to them and explain what it means; then pray with them about what you just discussed. Or take a story from the bible and put it in your own words at their understanding level. Don't dive too deep too soon with them; save the book of Revelation and all the charts for later.

2. **Keep it short** – Ten to fifteen minutes is about the maximum. Don't try to communicate too much for too long or you will lose their interest and their attention. Try to have a simple objective and drive it home. Remember that it is not how long that counts but how clear you make your point so they retain it.

3. **Keep it biblical** – Share stories of the Old Testament or basic truths of the New Testament. Such stories as Daniel in the lion's den; David slaying a lion, bear, and then Goliath; Esther becoming queen and saving a nation. These stories convey character, integrity, and commitment to God that you want to see developed in your children. Take simple scriptures from the New Testament to lay foundational truths. Share the parables of Jesus that speak of kingdom realities.

4. **Keep it fun** – Get animated in your story telling or use props. Have them dress up and become a part of the story. There are so many ways to make the bible come alive to your children. Ask the Holy Spirit to give you creative ideas and He will be faithful. My problem was I tended to get our kids over excited right before bedtime in my story telling making it difficult for Sue to get them calmed down and ready to sleep. However, my children still remember those storytelling times to this day and are passing it on to their children.

5. **End with prayer for them** – Now I'm not talking about three hours of intercessory prayer; do that in your own prayer time. Say simple short prayers for their siblings, extended family, friends. Speak over them to have a good night's sleep with dreams from God. Pray the scripture you read to them or the principle you want instilled in them. Come up with an easy-to-remember confession of faith that you repeat with them often. Have them pray

over their day. Again, you find out what works with your family and go with it!

The main thing in all of this is to emphasize God's love for them and how much you love them. God sent His own son to show us His love and to save us from our sin. Repeat this often! This might also be a good time to teach them the Lord's prayer:

After this manner therefore pray ye: Our Father which art in heaven, Hallowed be thy name. Thy kingdom come. Thy will be done in earth, as it is in heaven. Give us this day our daily bread. And forgive us our debts, as we forgive our debtors. And lead us not into temptation, but deliver us from evil: For thine is the kingdom, and the power, and the glory, for ever. Amen.

MATTHEW 6:9-13 (KJV)

Remember that if you have fun with it, they will look forward to this time together. Change it up at times, especially as they grow and mature and you are able to explain more. Don't let it become a religious habit but make it part of your life routine. They will be glad you did; specifically when they become parents themselves. Enjoy this time!

Father, thank You for saving me and
my house. I claim my children for Your
kingdom and divine purpose.
Thank You for revealing Yourself to them.

SALVATION

2 PETER 3:9 (NLT)

The Lord isn't really being slow about his promise, as some people think. No, he is being patient for your sake. He does not want anyone to be destroyed, but wants everyone to repent.

ACTS 16:31 (KJV)

And they said, Believe on the Lord Jesus Christ, and thou shalt be saved, and thy house.

JOHN 3:16 (KJV)

For God so loved the world, that he gave his only begotten Son, that whosoever believeth in him should not perish, but have everlasting life.

FRIENDSHIP

ECCLESIASTES 4:9-10 (KJV)

Two are better than one; because they have a good reward for their labour. For if they fall, the one will lift up his fellow: but woe to him that is alone when he falleth; for he hath not another to help him up.

I CORINTHIANS 15:33 (KJV)

Be not deceived: evil communications corrupt good manners.

PROVERBS 18:24 (KJV)

A man that hath friends must shew himself friendly: and there is a friend that sticketh closer than a brother.

PROVERBS 27:9 (KJV)

Ointment and perfume rejoice the heart: so doth the sweetness of a man's friend by hearty counsel.

Father, I thank You that my children demonstrate friendliness to their peers and that they are surrounded by friendly people. I thank You that their friendliness draws others to Christ, who is a friend closer than any brother.

Thank You, Father, for revealing Your kind of love to my children. I pray they get rooted and grounded in Your love. I pray they live a life of love for You and others. Show them how much I love, adore, and value them.

LOVE

EPHESIANS 3:17-19 (NLT)

Then Christ will make his home in your hearts as you trust in him. Your roots will grow down into God's love and keep you strong. And may you have the power to understand, as all God's people should, how wide, how long, how high, and how deep his love is. May you experience the love of Christ, though it is too great to understand fully. Then you will be made complete with all the fullness of life and power that comes from God.

1 CORINTHIANS 13:4-7 (NLT)

Love is patient and kind. Love is not jealous or boastful or proud or rude. It does not demand its own way. It is not irritable, and it keeps no record of being wronged. It does not rejoice about injustice but rejoices whenever the truth wins out. Love never gives up, never loses faith, is always hopeful, and endures through every circumstance.

JOY

JOB 5:17 (KJV)

Behold, happy is the man whom God correcteth: therefore despise not thou the chastening of the Almighty.

PSALM 128:1-2 (KJV)

Blessed is every one that feareth the Lord; that walketh in his ways. For thou shalt eat the labour of thine hands: happy shalt thou be, and it shall be well with thee.

I pray, Oh God, that my children fear and obey You. Thank you for Your happiness pursuing them in life. Thank You for the fruit of happiness in their lives.

Father, thank You that my children will walk in peace and not be contentious. Help them to avoid strife and make peace with men whenever possible. Help them not to be deceived by the world's definition of "peace", but to follow Godly peace in all areas of their lives.

PEACE

ROMANS 14:19 (KJV)

Let us therefore follow after the things which make for peace, and things wherewith one may edify another.

MATTHEW 5:9 (KJV)

Blessed are the peacemakers: for they shall be called the children of God.

ROMANS 12:18 (NLT)

Do all that you can to live in peace with everyone.

PATIENCE

HEBREWS 10:36 (NLT)

Patient endurance is what you need now, so that you will continue to do God's will. Then you will receive all that He has promised.

EPHESIANS 4:2 (NLT)

Always be humble and gentle. Be patient with each other, making allowance for each other's faults because of your love.

Father, I thank You that my children walk in patient endurance and will fulfill Your will for their lives. I pray that they will operate in love and patience towards others and be merciful towards their faults and in turn will reap mercy and patience from others.

Lord, help my children to be caring
and a comfort to others. Help them to model
kindness in everything they do.

KINDNESS

ROMANS 12:10 (NLT)

Love each other with genuine affection,
and take delight in honoring each other.

JOHN 11:19 (KJV)

And many of the Jews came to Martha and
Mary, to comfort them concerning their
brother.

EPHESIANS 4:32 (NLT)

Instead, be kind to each other, tenderhearted,
forgiving one another, just as God through
Christ has forgiven you.

GOODNESS

1 THESSALONIANS 5:15 (NLT)

*See that no one pays back evil for evil,
but always try to do good to each other
and to all people.*

ROMANS 12:9 (NLT)

*Don't just pretend to love others.
Really love them. Hate what is wrong.
Hold tightly to what is good.*

Father, thank You for Your goodness in my children's lives. Thank You that they will always seek to do good. Thank You that my children will love sincerely, walking after the precepts of the Lord. Thank You that goodness and mercy will follow them all the days of their lives.

FAITHFULNESS

LUKE 16:10 (KJV)

He that is faithful in that which is least is faithful also in much: and he that is unjust in the least is unjust also in much.

HEBREWS 10:25 (NLT)

And let us not neglect our meeting together, as some people do, but encourage one another, especially now that the day of his return is drawing near.

Father, I pray that my children be faithful to their relationship with You. Faithful in little things that You may make them rulers of much. I pray for my children to be committed and faithful to the church.

GENTLENESS

II TIMOTHY 2:24-25 (ASV)

And the Lord's servant must not strive, but be gentle towards all, apt to teach, forbearing in meekness correcting them that oppose themselves...

PSALMS 18:35 (GW)

You have given me the shield of salvation. Your right hand supports me. Your gentleness makes me great.

Father, thank You for my children being gentle in their approach towards others and that gentleness flowing through them will give them favor and they will walk in the greatness that You designed for them.

25

SELF-CONTROL (DISCIPLINE)

PROVERBS 25:28 (AMP)

Like a city that is broken down and without walls [leaving it unprotected] Is a man who has no self-control over his spirit [and sets himself up for trouble].

1 THESSALONIANS 5:6 (AMPC)

Accordingly then, let us not sleep, as the rest do, but let us keep wide awake (alert, watchful, cautious, and on our guard) and let us be sober (calm, collected, and circumspect).

Father, I pray my children develop self-control. Philippians 4:5 says to let Your moderation be known unto all men. Lord, show my children the value of living a prudent life, doing what is just and right by all men.

CONFIDENCE

PHILIPPIANS 4:13 (KJV)

I can do all things through Christ which strengtheneth me.

HEBREWS 10:35 (NLT)

So do not throw away this confident trust in the Lord. Remember the great reward it brings you!

Father, thank You, that through You, my children are ready for the challenges of life. My children are confident in Jesus and not arrogant or self-centered. I believe in Your divine plan for their life.

Thank You, Father, for helping my children grow in Your grace and knowledge. As they come to know You, they will love and be like You. Your grace is Your empowering presence, enabling them to be and do all You have ordained.

GROWING IN GRACE

2 PETER 3:18 (NLT)

Rather, you must grow in the grace and knowledge of our Lord and Savior Jesus Christ. All glory to him, both now and forever! Amen.

1 CORINTHIANS 15:10 (NLT)

But whatever I am now, it is all because God poured out his special favor on me— and not without results. For I have worked harder than any of the other apostles; yet it was not I but God who was working through me by his grace.

HONESTY & INTEGRITY

PSALM 25:21 (AMPC)

Let integrity and uprightness preserve me, for I wait for and expect You.

COLOSSIANS 3:9 (NLT)

Don't lie to each other, for you have stripped off your old sinful nature and all its wicked deeds.

Thank you, Father, for Your forgiveness toward my children through Your redemptive love. My children are forgiven as they surrender to God in worship and wonder. May my children be forgiving and kind in all they are involved in.

FORGIVING

EPHESIANS 4:32 (KJV)

And be ye kind one to another, tenderhearted, forgiving one another, even as God for Christ's sake hath forgiven you.

PSALM 130:4 (KJV)

But there is forgiveness with thee, that thou mayest be feared.

PROVERBS 10:12 (NLT)

Hatred stirs up quarrels, but love makes up for all offenses.

COURAGEOUS & STRONG

DEUTERONOMY 31:6 (KJV)

Be strong and of a good courage, fear not, nor be afraid of them: for the Lord thy God, He it is that doth go with thee; He will not fail thee, nor forsake thee.

JOSHUA 1:9 (ESV)

Have I not commanded you? Be strong and courageous. Do not be frightened, and do not be dismayed, for the Lord your God is with you wherever you go."

Fear has no place in my family. I bind fear of all kinds and release the spirit of a lion in my children. I pray they be bold, not rude, but bold as a lion.

PURITY

PSALM 51:10 (KJV)

Create in me a clean heart, O God; and renew a right spirit within me.

1 THESSALONIANS 4:3 (KJV)

For this is the will of God, even your sanctification, that ye should abstain from fornication.

MATTHEW 5:8 (KJV)

Blessed are the pure in heart: for they shall see God.

I pray that my children be pure in body and soul.
Help them keep thei... ...en
You and the... ...ord. I than... ...for
my children's freedom to enjoy... ...within the
cove...

Help me, Lord, to teach and model a good work ethic for my kids. Father, bless the work of my children's hands. I speak favor over their lives with God and man.

GOOD WORK ETHIC

COLOSSIANS 3:23 (KJV)

And whatsoever ye do, do it heartily, as to the Lord, and not unto men;

1 THESSALONIANS 4:11 (NLT)

Make it your goal to live a quiet life, minding your own business and working with your hands, just as we instructed you before.

EPHESIANS 4:28 (KJV)

Let him that stole steal no more: but rather let him labour, working with his hands the thing which is good, that he may have to give to him that needeth.

DEUTERONOMY 28:8 (KJV)

The Lord shall command the blessing upon thee in thy storehouses, and in all that thou settest thine hand unto; and He shall bless thee in the land which the Lord thy God giveth thee.

A SERVANT'S HEART

MATTHEW 20:27 (KJV)

And whosoever will be chief among you, let him be your servant.

EPHESIANS 6:8 (NLT)

Remember that the Lord will reward each one of us for the good we do, whether we are slaves or free.

2 SAMUEL 15:15 (KJV)

And the king's servants said unto the king, Behold, thy servants are ready to do whatsoever my lord the king shall appoint.

Thank You, Father, for a servant's heart in my children. May they think of others before themselves and over themselves. [...] joy of giving and [...] heart to serve

Father, my children will value Your Word and spiritual understanding. I pray Your Word becomes the final authority and absolute truth in their lives. I believe they will live by the principles and light of Your Word and thereby prosper.

LOVE FOR SCRIPTURES

PSALM 19:10 (KJV)

More to be desired are they than gold, yea, than much fine gold: sweeter also than honey and the honeycomb.

PSALM 119:105 (KJV)

Thy word is a lamp unto my feet, and a light unto my path.

PSALM 107:20 (KJV)

He sent his word, and healed them, and delivered them from their destructions.

Father, help my children to love justice as You do.

I pray they act justly in all they do.

Help them feel as You do when injustice

prevails. May they feel Your good pleasure when

righteousness prevails.

JUSTICE

PSALM 11:7 (NLT)

For the righteous LORD loves justice.
The virtuous will see His face.

MICAH 6:8 (KJV)

He hath shewed thee, O man, what is good;
and what doth the Lord require of thee, but
to do justly, and to love mercy, and to walk
humbly with thy God?

ISAIAH 1:17 (KJV)

Learn to do well; seek judgment, relieve the
oppressed, judge the fatherless, plead for the
widow.

SOUND JUDGMENT

JOHN 7:24 (KJV)

Judge not according to the appearance, but judge righteous judgment.

JAMES 2:12-13 (KJV)

So speak ye, and so do, as they that shall be judged by the law of liberty. For he shall have judgment without mercy, that hath shewed no mercy; and mercy rejoiceth against judgment.

Your Word declares You are known by judgments You execute (Psalm 9:16). May my children be remembered by good sense and judgment in their lives. Help my children to never judge by appearance or second-hand information, but make righteous judgments. I pray they make sound judgments in everything they do.

Father, I pray that my children are merciful, just as You are compassionate. May they sow mercy and reap a great harvest. Thank You that goodness and mercy will follow them all the days of their lives.

MERCY

LUKE 6:36 (KJV)

Be ye therefore merciful, as your Father also is merciful.

PROVERBS 11:17 (KJV)

The merciful man doeth good to his own soul: but he that is cruel troubleth his own flesh.

1 SAMUEL 24:17 (NLT)

And he said to David, "You are a better man than I am, for you have repaid me good for evil."

I pray all seven pillars of wisdom direct my children's lives: *Understanding; Justice; Judgment; Equity; Subtilty; Knowledge, and Discretion*. I pray all my children excel in wisdom and discernment and be full of the knowledge of the Lord.

WISDOM

PROVERBS 1:2-4 (KJV)

To know wisdom and instruction; to perceive the words of understanding; To receive the instruction of wisdom, justice, and judgment, and equity; To give subtilty to the simple, to the young man knowledge and discretion.

PROVERBS 8:11 (NLT)

For wisdom is far more valuable than rubies. Nothing you desire can compare with it.

PROVERBS 4:7 (KJV)

Wisdom is the principal thing; therefore get wisdom: and with all thy getting get understanding.

RESPECT FOR AUTHORITY

HEBREWS 13:7 (KJV)

Remember them which have the rule over you, who have spoken unto you the word of God: whose faith follow, considering the end of their conversation.

ROMANS 13:1-3 (NLT)

Everyone must submit to governing authorities. For all authority comes from God, and those in positions of authority have been placed there by God. So anyone who rebels against authority is rebelling against what God has instituted, and they will be punished. For the authorities do not strike fear in people who are doing right, but in those who are doing wrong. Would you like to live without fear of the authorities? Do what is right, and they will honor you.

I pray for a submissive heart and spirit for all my children. May they have proper respect for everyone. Thank You Lord for the great success and prosperity that will overtake them.

BIBLICAL ESTEEM

EPHESIANS 2:10 (KJV)

For we are his workmanship, created in Christ Jesus unto good works, which God hath before ordained that we should walk in them.

2 CORINTHIANS 5:17 (NLT)

This means that anyone who belongs to Christ has become a new person. The old life is gone; a new life has begun!

Help my children to see themselves as You see them (Your workmanship). Father, show them who they are in Christ and what they have and can do. I pray a HIGH CHRIST ESTEEM upon them. I pray they view all human life as valuable and precious.

PASSION FOR GOD

PSALM 63:8 (NLT)

I cling to You; Your strong right hand holds me securely.

PSALM 42:1-2 (KJV)

As the hart panteth after the water brooks, so panteth my soul after Thee, O God. My soul thirsteth for God, for the living God: when shall I come and appear before God?

HUMILITY

TITUS 3:2 (KJV)

To speak evil of no man, to be no brawlers, but gentle, shewing all meekness unto all men.

JAMES 4:10 (KJV)

Humble yourselves in the sight of the Lord, and He shall lift you up.

Father, help my children to speak evil of no one. Give them a spirit of gentleness and meekness toward all men. Thank You for lifting them up. Thank You for exalting them in due season.

COMPASSION

ZECHARIAH 7:9 (KJV)

Thus speaketh the Lord of hosts, saying, Execute true judgment, and shew mercy and compassions every man to his brother.

1 PETER 3:8 (KJV)

Finally, be ye all of one mind, having compassion one of another, love as brethren, be pitiful, be courteous.

1 JOHN 3:17 (KJV)

But whoso hath this world's good, and seeth his brother have need, and shutteth up his bowels of compassion from him, how dwelleth the love of God in him?

I pray my children learn compassion and to have empathy for others. May they be moved with God's love and be clothed with the virtue of tenderheartedness.

RESPONSIBILITY

GALATIANS 6:5 (AMP)

For every person will have to bear [with patience] his own burden [of faults and shortcomings for which he alone is responsible].

PROVERBS 4:23 (NLT)

Guard your heart above all else,
for it determines the course of your life.

PROVERBS 20:11 (KJV)

Even a child is known by his doings, whether
his work be pure, and whether it be right.

Father help my children to carry their own load.
My children will take responsibility for their lives
and actions. They will not play the blame game.

GENEROSITY

1 TIMOTHY 6:18-19 (KJV)

That they do good, that they be rich in good works, ready to distribute, willing to communicate; Laying up in store for themselves a good foundation against the time to come, that they may lay hold on eternal life.

LUKE 6:38 (NLT)

Give, and you will receive. Your gift will return to you in full—pressed down, shaken together to make room for more, running over, and poured into your lap. The amount you give will determine the amount you get back.

Father, thank You for giving my children a spirit of giving. I pray they learn to share and sow into others. It is a blessing to share and give, and they shall be blessed.

Lord give my children endurance and patience in all they do. May they always finish what they start. Help them never to give up, give in, or give out in their race.

ENDURANCE

HEBREWS 12:1 (KJV)

Wherefore seeing we also are compassed about with so great a cloud of witnesses, let us lay aside every weight, and the sin which doth so easily beset us, and let us run with patience the racè that is set before us,

HEBREWS 6:12 (NLT)

Then you will not become spiritually dull and indifferent. Instead, you will follow the example of those who are going to inherit God's promises because of their faith and endurance.

GALATIANS 6:9 (KJV)

And let us not be weary in well doing: for in due season we shall reap, if we faint not.

CONTENTMENT

PHILIPPIANS 4:12-13 (NLT)

I know how to live on almost nothing or with everything. I have learned the secret of living in every situation, whether it is with a full stomach or empty, with plenty or little. For I can do everything through Christ, who gives me strength.

1 TIMOTHY 6:6 (KJV)

But godliness with contentment is great gain.

Father teach my children the secret of being content in any and every situation through Him who gives them strength. Show them the significant gain of godliness with contentment.

71

Father, I pray for my children to operate in great faith. I thank You that my faith is generational. I pray for my children and grandchildren to walk in faith and please You. I pray You marvel at their faith versus unbelief.

GREAT FAITH

MATTHEW 8:10 (KJV)

When Jesus heard it, He marvelled, and said to them that followed, Verily I say unto you, I have not found so great faith, no, not in Israel.

MATTHEW 15:28 (NLT)

"Dear woman," Jesus said to her, "your faith is great. Your request is granted." And her daughter was instantly healed.

2 TIMOTHY 1:5 (NLT)

I remember your genuine faith, for you share the faith that first filled your grandmother Lois and your mother, Eunice. And I know that same faith continues strong in you.

PRAYER

EPHESIANS 6:18 (NLT)

Pray in the Spirit at all times and on every occasion. Stay alert and be persistent in your prayers for all believers everywhere.

PHILIPPIANS 4:6 (NLT)

Don't worry about anything; instead, pray about everything. Tell God what you need, and thank Him for all He has done.

1 THESSALONIANS 5:17 (KJV)

Pray without ceasing.

I pray for my children never to worry but learn to pray in all things. I pray for my children to know how to pray in the Spirit on all occasions with all kinds of prayers and requests.

SOCIAL MEDIA

1 CORINTHIANS 6:12 (KJV)

All things are lawful unto me, but all things are not expedient: all things are lawful for me, but I will not be brought under the power of any.

MATTHEW 10:16 (KJV)

Behold, I send you forth as sheep in the midst of wolves: be ye therefore wise as serpents, and harmless as doves.

Father, I pray my children are wise as serpents and harmless as doves. Thank you that my children know not everything available to them is good. Thank you that my children know your voice and another they will not follow.

SCRIPTURES TO CONFESS OVER OUR CHILDREN

ROMANS 12:2 (KJV)

And be not conformed to this world: but be ye transformed by the renewing of your mind, that ye may prove what is that good, and acceptable, and perfect, will of God.

1 CORINTHIANS 6:18-19 (KJV)

Flee fornication. Every sin that a man doeth is without the body; but he that committeth fornication sinneth against his own body. What? know ye not that your body is the temple of the Holy Ghost which is in you, which ye have of God, and ye are not your own?

PSALM 127:3 (KJV)

Lo, children are an heritage of the Lord: and the fruit of the womb is his reward.

PSALM 112:2 (KJV)

His seed shall be mighty upon earth: the generation of the upright shall be blessed.

MATTHEW 7:12 (NLT)

"Do to others whatever you would like them to do to you. This is the essence of all that is taught in the law and the prophets.

EPHESIANS 6:1-3 (KJV)

Children, obey your parents in the Lord: for this is right. Honour thy father and mother; (which is the first commandment with promise;) That it may be well with thee, and thou mayest live long on the earth.

1 TIMOTHY 4:12 (NLT)

Don't let anyone think less of you because you are young. Be an example to all believers in what you say, in the way you live, in your love, your faith, and your purity.

PSALM 138:8 (NLT)

The LORD will work out his plans for my life— for your faithful love, O LORD, endures forever. Don't abandon me, for you made me.

GENESIS 22:17 (NLT)

I will certainly bless you. I will multiply your descendants beyond number, like the stars in the sky and the sand on the seashore. Your descendants will conquer the cities of their enemies.

1 JOHN 4:4 (NLT)

But you belong to God, my dear children. You have already won a victory over those people, because the Spirit who lives in you is greater than the spirit who lives in the world.

GALATIANS 3:29 (NLT)

And now that you belong to Christ, you are the true children of Abraham. You are his heirs, and God's promise to Abraham belongs to you.

JEREMIAH 1:5 (NLT)

"I knew you before I formed you in your mother's womb. Before you were born I set you apart and appointed you as my prophet to the nations."

JEREMIAH 29:11 (NLT)

For I know the plans I have for you," says the LORD. "They are plans for good and not for disaster, to give you a future and a hope.

ISAIAH 59:21 (NLT)

"And this is my covenant with them," says the LORD. "My Spirit will not leave them, and neither will these words I have given you. They will be on your lips and on the lips of your children and your children's children forever. I, the LORD, have spoken!"

ROMANS 11:29 (NLT)

For God's gifts and his call can never be withdrawn.

ABOUT THE AUTHOR

Duane Sheriff is an apostolic teacher, international conference speaker, instructor at Charis Bible College, and the author of seven books: Rhythms of Grace, Erasing Offense, CounterCulture, Better Together, Our Union With Christ, Identity Theft, and Born Again, What Now? He is the Founding Pastor and Senior Elder of Victory Life, a multi-campus church headquartered in Durant, Oklahoma, where he served as Senior Pastor for over 35 years. Duane and his wife Sue have been married since 1980 and have four children and eleven precious grandchildren.

DSM

We exist to help people grow in Christ

Since 1983 we have been promoting the Word of God and helping people develop a personal relationship with Jesus. We have given away millions of teachings for free as cassette tapes, CD's and digital uploads. You can find all our free material online at **pastorduane.com**

It is only through the generosity of our Impact Partners that we are able to get the message of Grace & Truth out for free. If you've been blessed by this ministry, we would ask that you consider becoming a partner to help get these teachings to more people in need.

You can become a partner by visiting our website: **https://pastorduane.com/partnership**

or by calling the ministry at **580.634.5665**

www.ingramcontent.com/pod-product-compliance
Lightning Source LLC
Chambersburg PA
CBHW060345050426
42449CB00011B/2835